The Kids who Travel The WORLD

Paris

CANADIAN EXPAT MOM

Acknowledgements:

A giant thank you to my husband Kevin
who made our life in France possible,
and for supporting me while I decided that
this book needed to be written at the exact
same time as we moved our lives to the other
side of the planet. Never a dull moment!

For your eyes and feedback, thank you to
Shannon Day, Patsy Stadnyk and Lorraine Webb.

To Lourd Jim Diazon for joining me on this crazy book writing adventure.

Et à Sarah Arnold Darrigrand, merci pour ton aide précieuse et inattendue.
Tu es arrivée au moment idéal.

For my Daughters,

May you always be brave enough to embrace adventure, and strong enough to follow your hearts.

♡ Mom

The Kids That Travel The World
-Paris-
Written by: Lisa Stadnyk Webb
Illustrated by: Lourd Jim Diazon
www.canadianexpatmom.com
ISBN 978-602-73335-0-5
Text and Illustrations © Lisa Webb 2015

The Kids who Travel The World

Paris

Written by : Lisa Stadnyk Webb

Illustrated by : Lourd Jim Diazon

Infography by : Sarah Arnold Darrigrand

CANADIAN EXPAT MOM

Océane and Elodie are two sisters that have something very special in common.
They both love to travel the world.

The girls like helping each other pack their suitcases.

This time they were getting ready for an upcoming trip to Paris.

"We can't forget our passports!" their mom reminded them.

A passport is a special book with your picture inside that you need for travelling to new countries.

It also lets people know where you're from. Each time you enter a new country, your passport gets a stamp inside.

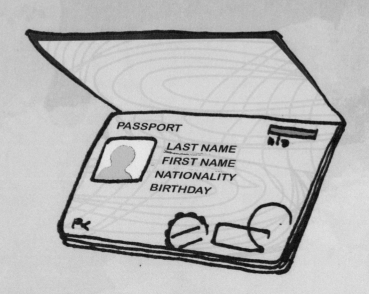

The girls were packed and ready to go to the airport.

On the plane Océane and Elodie made a list of all the things they wanted to see and do.

When they landed in Paris,
the capital city of France,
the girls were excited
to use some of the French
they had been practicing.

"**Bonjour!**" They used the French word for hello as they arrived at the taxi stand. They had already checked one item off their list. They were speaking French!

"**Merci!**" They said thank you in French as the taxi driver helped them with their luggage.

The girls looked out the window as they drove. The buildings were big, old, and beautiful.

Their mom told them that most people in Paris live in apartment buildings. They don't have back yards or gardens, so people meet their friends in neighbourhood parks to play and have picnics.

After dropping their suitcases off at the hotel, the two sisters wanted to see the Eiffel Tower. They had read that the tower lights up at night and at the top of every hour the lights twinkle brightly.

"Maybe that's why people call Paris the city of lights?"

Océane said to Elodie.

They woke up bright and early the next day and went exploring the streets of Paris. Before long they could smell something delicious. It was a *Boulangerie*. That means bakery in French.

Paris has many Boulangeries where they make fresh *baguettes*, *croissants*, and even bread with chocolate inside called *pain au chocolat*. The girls love chocolate so their choice was easy. The pain au chocolat was warm, delicious and left them both with chocolate mustaches.

"Dad, can we go for a ride on the Metro?"
Océane asked as they left the Boulangerie.

"Of course we can!"
her dad replied.

The Metro looks like a train, but it zooms below the streets of Paris.

Everyone went underground and got their tickets.

As they waited on the platform, they listened to a man playing music on the accordion.

Very quickly the Metro arrived and the doors opened. The sisters each held a parent's hand and went inside. What a fun ride! They had now checked off another item on their list.

The family got off the Metro and walked across the street into the *Jardin des Tuileries*. It was a big park, with fountains and lots of pigeons to chase around.
They loved it.

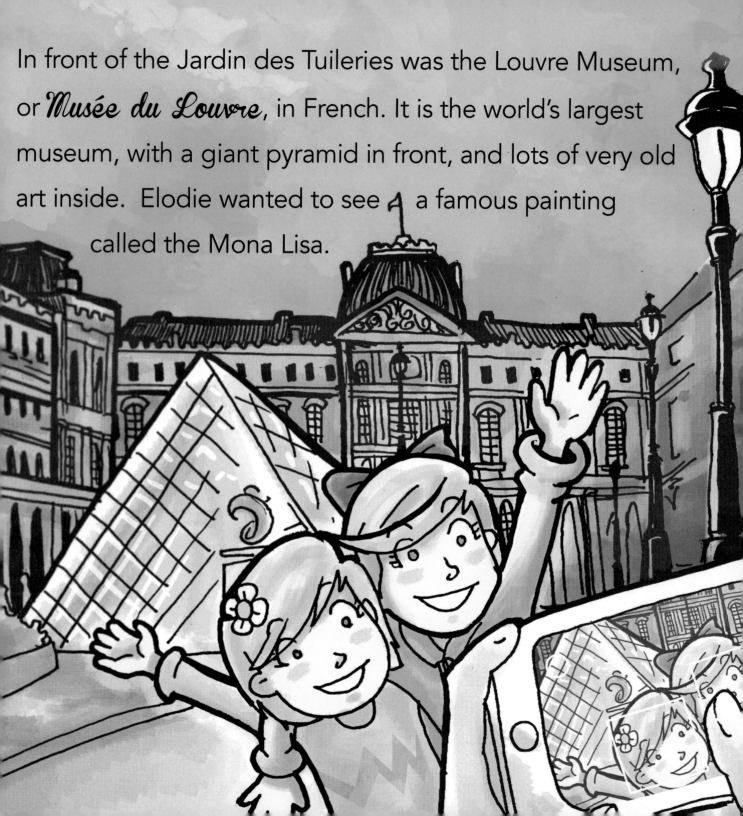

In front of the Jardin des Tuileries was the Louvre Museum, or *Musée du Louvre*, in French. It is the world's largest museum, with a giant pyramid in front, and lots of very old art inside. Elodie wanted to see a famous painting called the Mona Lisa.

$\mathcal{A}$fter exploring the Louvre all morning, they were hungry. The family went to a restaurant and sat at a table outside.

The girls giggled because someone had brought their pet dog to the restaurant and he was lying on the ground under the table.

Océane and Elodie decided to look over their list. Almost everything was checked off. They had learned some new French words, seen the Eiffel Tower, went to a Boulangerie, rode the Metro, and visited the Louvre. A lot of exploring had been done, but they were still missing one item from their list.

"We haven't walked on cobblestone streets yet."
Elodie said feeling disappointed.

"Of course you have" said their dad, "just look down."

Sure enough, the street they were walking on was made of big rocks, lined up beside each other to make the road. Many of the streets in France were made of cobblestone, the girls just hadn't noticed until now.

Time had passed quickly and their adventure in Paris was coming to an end.
The sisters managed to check everything off their list and were ready to fly back home.

…but not without making one more trip to the Boulangerie!

Océane (pronounced oh-say-an) and Elodie are French names. These two sisters are Canadian, but they were both born in France, where their family lived for 5 years.

They speak English with their "Mom" and French with their "Papa". The girls have been travelling the world together since they were born. Their family is now enjoying a new experience, living in Indonesia.

Join them on their adventures as they explore the globe and learn new things.

Made in the USA
Lexington, KY
21 January 2019